The Key on the Collar

By Elizabeth Van Steenwyk

Illustrated by Patricia Ludlow

Dominie Press, Inc.

Publisher: Raymond Yuen
Project Editor: John S. F. Graham
Editor: Bob Rowland
Designer: Greg DiGenti
Illustrator: Patricia Ludlow

Text Copyright © 2003 Elizabeth Van Steenwyk
Illustrations Copyright © 2003 Dominie Press, Inc.
All rights reserved. No part of this publication may
be reproduced or transmitted in any form or by any
means without permission in writing from the publisher.
Reproduction of any part of this book, through photocopy,
recording, or any electronic or mechanical retrieval system,
without the written permission of the publisher, is an
infringement of the copyright law.

Published by:

Dominie Press, Inc.
1949 Kellogg Avenue
Carlsbad, California 92008 USA

www.dominie.com

1-800-232-4570

Paperback ISBN 0-7685-2070-3
Printed in Singapore by PH Productions Pte Ltd
1 2 3 4 5 6 PH 05 04 03

Table of Contents

Chapter One
Sore Feet..5

Chapter Two
Mighty Important......................................10

Chapter Three
Ouch! 15

Chapter Four
Sniffing the Air..19

Chapter Five
Pepper..23

Chapter One
Sore Feet

The small, black dog limped slowly down the dusty road. As he walked, something clinked on his collar.

Clink. Clink. Clink.

He didn't notice the sound anymore. He was tired and hungry and lost.

Suddenly he smelled food. Fried chicken? Beef stew? Spaghetti? He liked everything. The dog hurried on sore feet toward the smell of food coming from the big yellow house.

Two brothers were playing catch in the front yard.

"Look at that ratty dog," the bigger boy said.

The smaller boy whistled. "Here boy!"

"Don't do that, Max," his brother yelled. "He could be mean."

"I'm only going to give him some water," Max answered. "He can't bite me when he's drinking."

Max filled a small bowl with water, and the dog quickly drank it all.

"Hey, Chad, listen," Max said. "Something on his collar is making a clinking sound."

"Maybe it's a medal for bravery," Chad said, laughing. "He followed *you*."

"You're not as funny as you look," Max said. He ran inside and came back with some food scraps in another bowl. The dog gulped down every bit and wagged his tail before he laid down in the grass.

"Max, what does it say on the dog's medal?"

Max bent down for a closer look. "It isn't a medal. It's a key."

"Why would a dog wear a key on his collar?" Chad wondered out loud.

"Search me," said Max. "You know, he looks really tired. Why don't we make a bed for him in the garage?" Max hurried on. "In the morning, maybe we can find out where he belongs."

They piled some old blankets together

and filled the water bowl again. After supper, they put more food scraps in a dish.

"Tomorrow, we have to figure out a name for you," Max said to the dog.

But in the morning, the dog was gone.

Chapter Two
Mighty Important

The dog walked down the road at daybreak. The road climbed a steep hill and entered a forest. The dog knew he had to go down the other side of the hill.

He climbed steadily until he reached a small cabin. The door was open, and he looked inside.

"Good morning," said a deep voice. "You're just in time for breakfast."

A heavy-set man with a long beard opened the door and the dog entered. He sat down beside the table and waited.

The old man went to the stove, spooned oatmeal into two bowls, and put one on the table and one on the floor. "Go on," he said. "It's good for you."

The dog hadn't eaten this stuff before, but he was hungry. The man ate, too, and then sat back to sip his coffee.

"Say, what is that thing on your collar?" he asked. "Is that your license tag?"

He leaned down to look. "Looks like a key I used to have, but I lost it." he said.

He thought a minute, and then got up and reached high onto a shelf. "Been meaning to break this strongbox open," he went on. "Maybe your key will open it, instead."

The old man removed the key from the dog's collar and tried it on his box. He tried again and again, but the lock wouldn't open. Finally, he put the key back on the collar.

"That key must be mighty important, since someone trusted it to you," the old man said, sitting down once again.

The dog walked to the screen door. He wagged his tail and waited.

"I see," the old man said. "You've got somewhere to go, and someone is waiting for that key."

He got up from the chair, reached down, and gave the dog a pat. "Thanks for coming by and keeping me company a little while."

He opened the screen door, and the

dog walked down the path, deeper into the woods. The forest was very quiet, except for the *clink, clink, clink* of the key on the dog's collar.

Chapter Three
Ouch!

The day grew hot, and the dog became very thirsty. He thought he smelled water and ran toward it. He searched for the water under some weeds. Ouch! He stuck his nose in a thistle. The dog shook his head, but couldn't get the thistle off his nose.

Slowly, he walked on. His nose throbbed. By sundown, he reached the other side of the forest. He stopped when he saw the house with blue shutters.

The front door opened, and a little girl stepped outside.

"Don't go far, Polly," a voice called from inside the house.

Polly saw the dog with a thistle stuck on his nose.

"You poor thing," she said. "Come with me." The dog followed her to an old shed. "This is my magic castle," she said. "I can fix anything here."

They went inside and she lit a small candle. "Sit here," she said. "Now I'm going to say the magic words and you will be just fine. She closed her eyes and wiggled her nose.

"Witches, itches, broom, and bristle. Take away the hurting thistle."

She pulled it out. That felt so much better. The dog shook himself and stood up.

"What's that on your collar?" the girl asked. She gasped. "Oh, my, I think it's my missing key! If it is, you are my missing magic dog!"

Quickly, she removed the dog's collar and ran to the door. She tried the key in the lock, but it didn't work. Nothing happened.

"Oh, well. I guess it isn't my key, after all," she said. "Now you will have to leave. Only the one who has my missing magic key may stay with me."

She opened the door, and the dog trotted outside. Night was coming. It was getting darker. And he was really lost!

Chapter Four
Sniffing the Air

The dog walked all night. Toward daylight he came to the edge of a village. He was hungry and tired, but something made him go on. He came to the town square. Stores were closed. No one strolled through the park.

The dog sniffed the air. He followed the strong smell. He stopped at a trashcan and sniffed again. Smoke curled out of the can. He had been smelling smoke. The dog began to bark to alert people to the danger.

A door opened across the street. "What's all the fuss about?" said a young man. Then he saw the smoke.

"Thanks for the warning!" he said. A couple of seconds later, he hurried over to put out the fire with a bucket of water.

"You're a good fire alarm," said the young man, bending down to pet the dog. "We can use you at the fire station. Come on." They crossed the street and went inside. *Clink, clink, clink* went the key on the dog's collar.

"Hey, everybody, I've got a new fire alarm," the young man said. "Let's give

him some breakfast. He earned it."

They placed a dish full of bacon and eggs and pancakes in front of the small, black dog, and he ate every crumb. Then he curled up on an old rug for a nap.

His new friend bent down to pet him. "I keep hearing a funny clinking sound when you move," he said. "Now I see what it is. It's a key."

A couple of the other firefighters came over to admire the dog. "What do you think that key is for?" one of them said.

"Doesn't look like a car key," said another. "How about a kid's play house?"

"Could it be for a safe deposit box at the bank?" another firefighter asked.

"No," the others said together.

Suddenly, the dog stood up. He sniffed the air. Now he smelled something else. Something very familiar. He walked to the front door that opened to the square.

He wagged his tail excitedly. He scratched the door. He whined. He had to get outside as fast as he could.

Chapter Five
Pepper

The dog looked from left to right. No one strolled the streets yet. But he knew someone special had been there.

He hurried to the corner and looked up and down the street. There, just turning a corner ahead, was a boy on a bicycle. Yes! He knew that bike.

He ran fast. Faster. But he couldn't catch up. The boy slowed down at the intersection. Then he turned left.

The street led to a neighborhood with small houses and large trees. He knew those houses. He knew those trees.
The dog began to pant hard as he ran, keeping his eyes on the bicycle. Then the bike turned a corner. But by the time he reached it, the boy and the bike had disappeared.

But it didn't matter! Now the dog knew where he was.

He barked and barked as he ran down the street and headed into a familiar driveway.

"Pepper!" Joey yelled. He was just getting off his bicycle. "You found us!" He ran to the dog, and they hugged each other.

Joey's mom and dad and sister hurried out of the house. The door slammed behind them.

"We thought you were lost on our camping trip," said Joey's sister, Carolyn. "Lost forever."

"He's been traveling hard," Dad said. "Let's go inside and fix his paws."

"Guess we'll have to use his key then," Mom said. "The wind slammed the door shut, and now we're locked out again."

Joey took off Pepper's collar and unlocked the back door with the key.

"That spare key was meant for us to use in an emergency," Dad said.

"Pepper arrived just in time," Joey said. "I wish he could tell us where he's been."

"I'm just glad he's here," said Carolyn. "And I think he's glad, too."

As Pepper barked, the key on his collar clinked and clinked and clinked. He was really happy to be home again.

Author's Note: *Our dog, Freckles, wore the back door key on his collar for years, helping our family through several emergencies.*